Hannah's Four Seasons

Bill Francis

ROSEN
COMMON CORE
READERS

Rosen
Classroom™

New York

Published in 2013 by The Rosen Publishing Group, Inc.
29 East 21st Street, New York, NY 10010

Book Design: Michael Harmon

Photo Credits: Cover Steve Dunwell/Photographer's Choice/Getty Images; pp. 4, 8 (snowy tree) rolfo/Flickr/
Getty Images; pp. 4, 12, 14 (beach) Dougal Waters/Iconica/Getty Images; p. 4 (fall leaves) Digital Vision/Digital
Vision/Getty Images; p. 4 (spring buds) Kelly Sillaste/Flickr/Getty Images; p. 5 (sleds) Laurie Rubin/The Image Bank/
Getty Images; p. 5 (pails) Anthony-Masterson/Botanica/Getty Images; pp. 5, 7 (rake) Victoria Pearson/
The Image Bank/Getty Images; p. 5 (puddle) Armadillo Stock/Shutterstock.com; pp. 6, 14 (fall leaves) Photodisc/
Photodisc/Getty Images; pp. 9, 14 (snowman) David De Lossy/Photodisc/Getty Images; pp. 10, 14 (rain flowers)
Cornelia Doerr/Photographer's Choice RF/Getty Images; p. 11 Elena Litsova Photography/Flickr/Getty Images;
p. 13 Thomas Barwick/Iconica/Getty Images.

ISBN: 978-1-4488-8740-8
6-pack ISBN: 978-1-4488-8741-5

Manufactured in the United States of America

CPSIA Compliance Information: Batch #WS12RC: For further information contact Rosen Publishing, New York, New York at 1-800-237-9932.

Word Count: 103

Contents

Hannah likes all the seasons of the year.

She finds things to do during every season.

The air is cool in fall.

Leaves change color and fall to the ground.

Hannah likes to rake leaves during fall.

It is cold in winter.

The ground is covered in snow.

Hannah likes to build snowmen
during winter.

The ground is wet in spring.
Birds sing and flowers grow.

Hannah likes to jump in puddles during spring.

The sun is warm in summer.
There is no school!

Hannah likes to swim during summer.

Hannah loves all the seasons!
Do you have a season you like best?

Know the Seasons

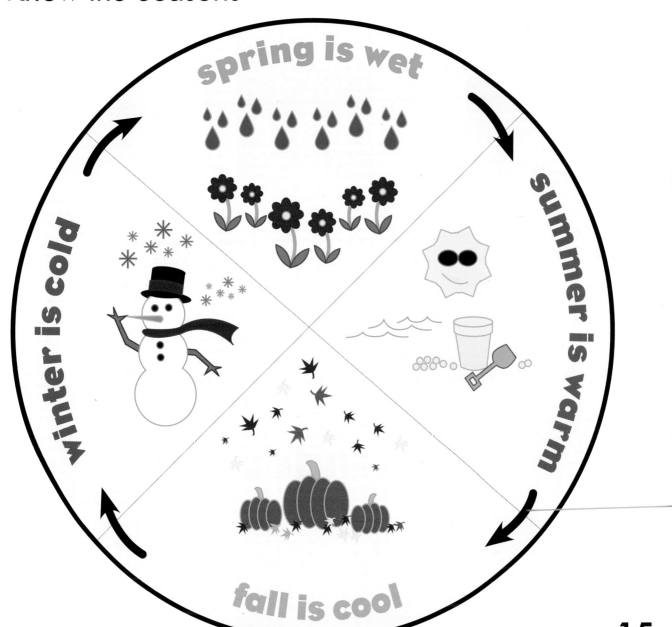

spring is wet

summer is warm

fall is cool

winter is cold

Words to Know

ground

leaves

puddles

snow

swimming

Index